KETO CHAFFLE RECIPES

LOSE WEIGHT, FEEL GREAT, STAY IN KETOSIS, AND EAT SUPER TASTY WAFFLES – SIMPLE–TO– MAKE KETO WAFFLE RECIPES FOR ANYONE

Megan Slim

TABLE OF CONTENT

The following Book is reproduced below with the goal of providing information that is as accurate and reliable as possible. Regardless, purchasing this Book can be seen as consent to the fact that both the publisher and the author of this book are in no way experts on the topics discussed within and that any recommendations or suggestions that are made herein are for entertainment purposes only. Professionals should be consulted as needed prior to undertaking any of the action endorsed herein.

This declaration is deemed fair and valid by both the American Bar Association and the Committee of Publishers Association and is legally binding throughout the United States. Furthermore, the transmission, duplication, or reproduction of any of the following work including specific information will be considered an illegal act irrespective of if it is done electronically or in print. This extends to creating a secondary or tertiary copy of the work or a recorded copy and is only allowed with the express written consent from the Publisher. All additional right reserved.

The information in the following pages is broadly considered a truthful and accurate account of facts and as such, any inattention, use, or misuse of the information in question by the reader will render any resulting actions solely under their purview. There are no scenarios in which the publisher or the original author of this work can be in any fashion deemed liable for any hardship or damages that may befall them after undertaking information described herein.

Additionally, the information in the following pages is intended only for informational purposes and should thus be thought of as universal. As befitting its nature, it is presented without assurance regarding its prolonged validity or interim quality. Trademarks that are mentioned are done without written consent and can in no way be considered an endorsement from the trademark holder.

INTRODUCTION

You might have heard someone talking about eating chaffles, but you're not quite sure what it is. Chaffles are a tasty dish that combines two of the most delicious foods of all time—waffles and pancakes. If you love getting breakfast for dinner, then you'll love chaffles even more. These tasty treats are incredibly simple to make. The reason chaffles are so yummy is that waffles and pancakes both contain a lot of butter, which makes them rich in flavor. The syrup really brings out the flavor of both the waffles and the pancakes, just as it does when spread over maple waffles or on top of a stack of flapjacks.

A chaffle requires no special equipment or ingredients to prepare. However, if you plan to make these tasty treats often, you may want to pick up some extra equipment. You'll need a waffle iron, which again can be found at any large grocery store for less than $30. And finally, you'll want a giant pair of tongs. This tool has several different functions and will come in handy when you're making chaffles or even some other dishes—it's really a multipurpose kitchen utensil.

The slotted side is meant for removing ice from drinks, while the other side is meant for chopping food.

You can use the tongs to slide your chaffle off of the waffle iron or to flip it once it's folded. If you enjoy chaffles, you might want to try some of the other tasty, delicious dish recipes in this series.

Crepes and waffles are a fantastic combination; in fact, many chefs like to combine these two foods to create common dishes. You can really experiment with all kinds of food combinations with crepes and waffles—they are an incredibly versatile food group!

Chaffles are really a great way to bring together two classic dishes into one fabulous meal. If you're a big fan of breakfast food, then you will absolutely love chaffles. All you need to prepare these tasty treats is a waffle iron and some pancake batter. Serve your chaffles with butter and syrup for a special breakfast treat – your family may even ask for seconds!

1.Keto Chocolate Twinkie Copycat Chaffle

🍴 **Servings**: 2

🥄 **Preparation Time**: 5 Minutes

⏰ **Cooking Time**: 12 Minutes

📋 ## Ingredients :

- ❖ 2 tablespoons of butter (cooled)

- ❖ 2 oz. Cream cheese softened

- ❖ Two large egg room temperature

- ❖ 1 teaspoon of vanilla essence

- ❖ 1/4 cup Lakanto confectionery

- ❖ A pinch of pink salt

- ❖ 1/4 cup almond flour

- ❖ 2 tablespoons coconut powder

- ❖ 2 tablespoons cocoa powder

- ❖ 1 teaspoon baking powder

Directions:

1. Preheat the Maker of Corndog.

2. Melt the butter for a minute and let it cool.

3. In the butter, whisk the eggs until smooth.

4. Remove sugar, cinnamon, sweetener and blend well.

5. Add almond flour, coconut flour, cacao powder, and baking powder.

6. Blend until well embedded.

7. Fill each well with two tablespoons of batter and spread evenly.

8. Close the lid and let it cook for 4 minutes.

9. Lift from the rack and cool it down.

Nutrition: Calories: 104; **Total Fat**: 6.2g;

Cholesterol: 67.1mg; **Sodium**: 485.5mg;

Total Carbohydrates: 5.3g; **Dietary Fiber**: 1.7g; **Sugars**: 1.6g;

Protein: 4.4g; **Vitamin A**: 80.1μg; **Vitamin C**: 0mg

2. Keto Chaffle Stuffing

✗ Servings: 2

✎ Preparation Time: 20 Minutes

⏰ Cooking Time: 40 Minutes

📋 *Ingredients* :

-Basic chaffle ingredients:

- ❖ 1/2 cup cheese mozzarella, cheddar cheese, or a combination of both

- ❖ 2 eggs

- ❖ 1/4 teaspoon of garlic powder

- ❖ 1/2 teaspoon onion powder

- ❖ 1/2 teaspoon dried chicken seasoning

- ❖ 1/4 teaspoon salt

- ❖ 1/4 teaspoon pepper

Ingredients: -for filling:

- ❖ 1 Diced onion

- ❖ 2 Celery stems

- ❖ 4 oz. Mushrooms diced

- ❖ 4 cups of butter for sautéing

- ❖ 3 eggs

Directions:

1. First, make a chaffle. This recipe makes four mini-chaffles.

2. Preheat the mini waffle iron.

3. Preheat oven to 350°F

4. In a medium bowl, mix the chaffle ingredients.

5. Pour 1/4 of the mixture into a mini waffle maker and cook each chaffle for about four minutes.

6. Once cooked, set them aside.

7. In a small skillet, fry the onions, celery, and mushrooms until soft.

8. In a separate bowl, split the chaffle into small pieces and add sautéed vegetables and three eggs. Mix until the ingredients are completely bonded.

9. Add the mixture of fillings to a small casserole dish (about 4x4) and bake at 350 degrees for about 30-40 minutes.

Note: Make four chaffles.

Nutrition: Calories: 229; Total Fat: 17.6g

Cholesterol: 265.6mg; **Sodium:** 350mg

Total Carbohydrates: 4.6g; **Dietary Fiber:** 1.1g

Sugars: 2g; **Protein:** 13.7g; **Vitamin A:** 217.2µg

Vitamin C: 2.4mg

3. Keto Cornbread Chaffle

🍴 **Servings**: 2

🥄 **Preparation Time**: 5 Minutes

⏰ **Cooking Time**: 5 Minutes

📋 ## *Ingredients*:

- ❖ 1 egg

- ❖ 1/2 cup shredded cheddar cheese (or mozzarella cheese)

- ❖ 5 Slices Jalapeno (optional) freshly picked or fresh

- ❖ 1 teaspoon of Frank's Red-Hot Sauce

- ❖ 1/4 teaspoon corn extract as an essential secret ingredient!

- ❖ A pinch of salt

Directions:

1. Preheat the Mini waffle maker, place the eggs in a small bowl.

2. Add the remaining ingredients and combine until well absorbed.

3. Apply one tablespoon of shredded cheese to the waffle maker for 30 seconds before removing the mixture. It produces a very clean and friendly crust!

4. Add half of the mixture to the preheated waffle maker.

5. Cook for a total of 3-4 minutes. The more they remain, the crunchier.

6. Enjoy it served warm!

Nutrition: Calories: 150; Total Fat: 11.8g

Cholesterol: 121mg; **Sodium**: 1399.4mg

Total Carbohydrates: 1.1g; **Dietary Fiber**: 0g

Sugars: 0.2g; **Protein**: 9.6g; **Vitamin A**: 134.1µg

Vitamin C: 0.1mg

4. Maple Pumpkin Keto Chaffle

Servings: 2

Preparation Time: 5 Minutes

Cooking Time: 4 Minutes

📋 *Ingredients :*

- ❖ 3/4 teaspoon baking powder

- ❖ 2 eggs

- ❖ 4 teaspoons heavy whipping cream

- ❖ 1/2 cup mozzarella cheese, shredded

- ❖ 2 teaspoons Liquid Stevia

- ❖ A pinch of salt

- ❖ 3/4 teaspoons pumpkin pie spice

- ❖ 1 teaspoon coconut flour

- ❖ 2 teaspoons pumpkin puree (100% pumpkin)

- ❖ 1/2 teaspoons vanilla

Directions:

1. Preheat the mini waffle maker until hot

2. Whisk the egg in a bowl, add cheese, and then mix well

3. Stir in the remaining ingredients (except toppings, if any).

4. Scoop 1/2 of the batter onto the waffle maker, spread across evenly

5. Cook 3-4 minutes, until done as desired (or crispy).

6. Gently remove from the waffle maker and let it cool

7. Repeat with the remaining batter.

8. Top with sugar-free maple syrup or keto ice cream.

9. Serve and Enjoy!

Nutrition: Calories: 201; Net carbs: 2g   Fat: 15g;
Protein: 12g

5.   Keto Almond Blueberry Chaffle

🍴 **Servings:** 2

🥄 **Preparation Time**: 5 Minutes

⏰ **Cooking Time**: 5 Minutes

📋 Ingredients:

❖ 1 teaspoon baking powder

❖ 2 eggs

❖ 1 cup of mozzarella cheese

❖ 2 tablespoons almond flour

❖ 3 tablespoons blueberries

❖ 1 teaspoon cinnamon

❖ 2 teaspoons of Swerve

Directions:

1. Preheat the mini waffle maker until hot

2. Whisk egg in a bowl, add cheese, and then mix well

3. Stir in the remaining ingredients (except toppings, if any).

4. Grease the preheated waffle maker with non-stick cooking spray.

5. Scoop 1/2 of the batter onto the waffle maker, spread across evenly

6. Cook until a bit browned and crispy, about 4 minutes.

7. Cook 3-4 minutes, until done as desired (or crispy).

8. Gently remove from the waffle maker and let it cool

9. Repeat with the remaining batter.

10. Top with keto syrup

11. Serve and Enjoy!

Nutrition: Calories: 116; Net carbs: 1g   Fat: 8g;

Protein: 8g

6. Keto Breakfast Chaffle

🍴 **Servings**: 1

🥄 **Preparation Time**: 3 Minutes

⏰ **Cooking Time**: 6 Minutes

Ingredients:

- ❖ 2 tablespoons butter

- ❖ 1 egg

- ❖ 1/2 cup Monterey Jack Cheese

- ❖ 1 tablespoon almond flour

Directions:

1. Preheat the mini waffle maker until hot

2. Whisk the egg in a bowl, add cheese, and then mix well

3. Stir in the remaining ingredients (except toppings, if any).

4. Grease the waffle maker and Scoop 1/2 of the batter onto the waffle maker, spread across evenly

5. Cook until a bit browned and crispy, about 4 minutes.

6. Gently remove from the waffle maker and let it cool

7. Repeat with the remaining batter.

8. Melt butter in a pan. Add chaffles to the pan and cook for 2 minutes on each side

9. Remove from the pan and let it cool.

10. Serve and Enjoy!

Nutrition: Calories: 257; **Net carbs:** 1g; **Fat:** 24g; **Protein:** 11g

7. Sweet Cinnamon "Sugar" Chaffle

X **Servings**: 1

Preparation Time: 5 Minutes

Cooking Time: 4 Minutes

Ingredients:

- ❖ 1/2 teaspoon cinnamon (topping)

- ❖ 10 Drops of liquid Stevia

- ❖ 1 tablespoon almond flour

- ❖ Two large eggs

- ❖ A splash of vanilla

- ❖ 1/2 cup mozzarella cheese

Directions:

1. Preheat the waffle maker until hot

2. Whisk egg in a bowl, add cheese, and then mix well

3. Stir in the remaining ingredients (except toppings, if any).

4. Scoop 1/2 of the batter onto the waffle maker, spread across evenly

5. Cook 3-4 minutes, until done as desired (or crispy).

6. Gently remove from the waffle maker and let it cool

7. Repeat with the remaining batter.

8. Top with melted butter and a sprinkle of cinnamon.

9. Serve and Enjoy!

Nutrition: Calories: 221; Net carbs: 2g; Fat: 17g; Protein: 12g

8. Keto "Cinnamon Roll" Chaffles

✗ **Servings**: 2

🖊 **Preparation Time**: 5 Minutes

⏰ **Cooking Time**: 10 Minutes

📋 ## Ingredients:

Cinnamon Roll Chaffle:

- ❖ 1/2 cup mozzarella cheese

- ❖ 1/4 teaspoon baking powder

- ❖ 1 teaspoon Granulated Swerve

- ❖ 1 tablespoon almond flour

- ❖ 1 teaspoon cinnamon

- ❖ 1 egg

Cinnamon Roll Swirl:

❖ 2 teaspoons confectioners swerve

❖ 1 tablespoon butter

❖ 1 teaspoon cinnamon

Keto Cinnamon Roll Glaze:

❖ 2 teaspoons swerve confectioners

❖ 1/4 teaspoons vanilla extract

❖ 1 tablespoon cream cheese

❖ 1 tablespoon butter

Directions:

1. Preheat the waffle maker until hot

2. Add Cinnamon roll chaffle ingredients in a bowl and combine well

3. In another small bowl, add the cinnamon Roll Swirl ingredients, and stir well.

4. Microwave for 15 seconds and mix well.

5. Spray the waffle maker with non-stick spray and add 1/3 of the batter to your waffle maker.

6. Swirl in 1/3 of the "cinnamon roll swirl ingredients" mixture on top of it.

7. Cook for 3-4 minutes. Repeat for the remaining batter.

8. In a small bowl, add "Keto cinnamon roll glaze ingredients," combine and microwave for 20 seconds.

9. Drizzle on top of the chaffles

Nutrition: Calories: 180; Net carbs: 1g; Fat: 16g; Protein: 7g

9. Pizza Flavored Chaffle

✗ **Servings**: 2

🥄 **Preparation Time**: 6 Minutes

⏰ **Cooking Time**: 12 Minutes

📋 *Ingredients*:

- ❖ 1 egg, beaten

- ❖ ½ cup cheddar cheese, shredded

- ❖ 2 tablespoons pepperoni, chopped

- ❖ 1 tablespoon keto marinara sauce

- ❖ 4 tablespoons almond flour

- ❖ 1 teaspoon baking powder

- ❖ ½ teaspoon dried Italian seasoning

- ❖ Parmesan cheese, grated

Directions:

1. Preheat your waffle maker.

2. In a bowl, mix the egg, cheddar cheese, pepperoni, marinara sauce, almond flour, baking powder, and Italian seasoning.

3. Add the mixture to the waffle maker.

4. Close the device and cook for some minutes.

5. Open it and transfer the chaffle to a plate.

6. Let cool for 2 minutes.

7. Repeat the steps with the remaining batter.

8. Top with the grated parmesan and serve.

Nutrition: Calories: 17; Total Fat: 14.3g;

Saturated Fat: 7.5g; **Cholesterol:** 118mg; **Sodium:** 300mg;

Potassium: 326mg; **Total Carbohydrates**: 1.8g;

Dietary Fiber: 0.1g; **Protein**: 11.1g; **Total Sugars**: 0.4g

10. Maple Chaffle

Servings: 2

Preparation Time: 10 Minutes

Cooking Time: 15 Minutes

Ingredients:

- ❖ 1 egg, lightly beaten

- ❖ 2 egg whites

- ❖ 1/2 teaspoon maple extract

- ❖ 2 teaspoons Swerve

- ❖ 1/2 teaspoon baking powder, gluten-free

- ❖ 2 tablespoons almond milk

- ❖ 2 tablespoons coconut flour

Directions:

1. Preheat your waffle maker.

2. In a bowl, whisk egg whites until stiff peaks form.

3. Stir in maple extract, Swerve, baking powder, almond milk, coconut flour, and egg.

4. Spray waffle maker with cooking spray.

5. Introduce half batter in the hot waffle maker and cook for 3-minutes or until golden brown. Repeat with the remaining batter.

6. Serve and enjoy.

Nutrition: Calories: 122; Fat: 6.6 **Carbohydrates**: 9; Sugar: 1; **Protein**: 7; **Cholesterol**: 82mg

11. Creamy Chaffles

X **Servings:** 2

Preparation Time: 8 Minutes

Cooking Time: 5 Minutes

Ingredients:

- ❖ 1 cup egg whites

- ❖ 1 cup cheddar cheese, shredded

- ❖ 2 oz. Cocoa powder.

- ❖ 1 Pinch salt

Topping:

- ❖ 4 oz. Cream cheese

- ❖ Strawberries

- ❖ Blueberries

❖ Coconut flour

Directions:

1. Beat the egg whites until fluffy and white

2. Chop Italian cheese with a knife and beat with egg whites.

3. Add cocoa powder and salt in the mixture and again beat.

4. Spray non-stick cooking spray into a round waffle maker.

5. Pour some batter into the waffle maker.

6. Cook the chaffle for about 5 minutes.

7. Once cooked, carefully remove the chaffle from the maker.

8. For serving, spread cream cheese on a chaffle. Top with strawberries, blueberries, and coconut flour.

9. Serve and enjoy!

Nutrition: Protein: 68; Fat: 187; Carbohydrates: 9

12. Choco and Spinach Chaffles

✘ **Servings**: 2

🥄 **Preparation Time**: 10 Minutes

⏰ **Cooking Time**: 5 Minutes

📋 *Ingredients* :

- ❖ 1 tablespoon. almond flour

- ❖ ½ cup chopped spinach

- ❖ 1/2 cup cheddar cheese

- ❖ 1 tablespoon cocoa powder

- ❖ ½ teaspoon baking powder

- ❖ 1 Large egg.

- ❖ 2 tablespoons Almond butter

❖ 1/2 teaspoon salt

❖ 1/2 teaspoon pepper

Directions:

1. Start by preheating the waffle iron

2. Blend all ingredients in a blender until mixed.

3. Pour 1/8 cup cheese into a waffle maker, and then pour the mixture into the greased waffle center.

4. Again, sprinkle cheese on the batter.

5. Cover.

6. Cook chaffles for about 4-5 minutes until cooked and crispy.

7. Once chaffles are cooked, remove and enjoy.

Nutrition: Protein: 4; Fat: 128; Carbohydrates: 11

13. Pumpkin Chaffles With Choco Chips

✗ **Servings**: 2

🥄 **Preparation Time**: 6 Minutes

⏰ **Cooking Time**: 12 Minutes

📋 *Ingredients*:

- ❖ 1 egg

- ❖ ½ cup shredded mozzarella cheese

- ❖ 4 teaspoons pureed pumpkin

- ❖ ¼ teaspoon pumpkin pie spice

- ❖ 2 tablespoons sweetener

- ❖ 1 tablespoon almond flour

- ❖ 4 teaspoons chocolate chips (sugar-free)

Directions:

1. Turn your waffle maker on.

2. In a bowl, beat the egg and stir in the pureed pumpkin.

3. Mix well.

4. Add the rest of the ingredients one by one.

5. Pour 1/3 of the mixture into your waffle maker.

6. Cook for 4 minutes.

7. Repeat the same steps with the remaining mixture.

Nutrition: Calories: 93; Total Fat: 7; Saturated Fat: 3;

Cholesterol: 69mg; Sodium: 13mg; Potassium: 48mg

Total Carbohydrates: 2; Dietary Fiber: 1; Protein: 7g; Total

Sugars: 1g

14. Red Velvet Chaffle

✗ **Servings:** 2

🥄 **Preparation Time**: 6 Minutes

⏰ **Cooking Time**: 12 Minutes

📋 *Ingredients* :

- ❖ 1 egg

- ❖ ¼ cup mozzarella cheese, shredded

- ❖ 1 oz. Cream cheese

- ❖ 4 tablespoons almond flour

- ❖ 1 teaspoon baking powder

- ❖ 2 teaspoons sweetener

- ❖ 1 teaspoon red velvet extract

- ❖ 2 tablespoons cocoa powder

Directions:

1. Combine all the ingredients in a bowl.

2. Plug your waffle maker in.

3. Pour some batter into the waffle maker.

4. Seal and cook for four minutes.

5. Open and transfer to a plate.

6. Repeat the steps with the remaining batter.

Nutrition: Calories: 126; Total Fat: 10.1g

Saturated Fat: 3.4g; **Cholesterol:** 66mg; **Sodium**: 68mg;

Potassium: 290mg; **Total Carbohydrates**: 6.5g;

Dietary Fiber: 2.8g; **Protein:** 5.9g; **Total Sugars**: 0.2g

15. Walnuts Low Carb Chaffles

🍴 **Servings**: 2

🥄 **Preparation Time**: 10 Minutes

⏰ **Cooking Time**: 5 Minutes

📋 ## Ingredients:

❖ 2 tablespoons Cream cheese

- ❖ $\frac{1}{2}$ teaspoon almonds flour

- ❖ $\frac{1}{4}$ teaspoon baking powder

- ❖ 1 Large egg

- ❖ $\frac{1}{4}$ cup chopped walnuts

- ❖ A pinch of stevia extract powder

Directions:

1. Preheat your waffle maker.

2. Spray the waffle maker with cooking spray.

3. In a bowl, add cream cheese, almond flour, baking powder, egg, walnuts, and Stevia.

4. Mix all ingredients.

5. Spoon the walnut batter in the waffle maker and cook for about 2-3 minutes.

6. Let chaffles cool at room temperature before serving.

Nutrition: Protein: 12%; Fat: 80%

Carbohydrates: 8%

16. Chaffle Cream Cake

✗ **Servings**: 2

🥄 **Preparation Time**: 10 Minutes

⏰ **Cooking Time**: 30 Minutes

📋 Ingredients : Chaffle:

❖ 4 oz. Cream cheese

❖ 4 eggs

❖ 1 tablespoon butter, melted

❖ 1 teaspoon vanilla extract

❖ ½ teaspoon cinnamon

❖ 1 tablespoon sweetener

❖ 4 tablespoons coconut flour

❖ 1 tablespoon almond flour

- ❖ 1 ½ teaspoons baking powder

- ❖ 1 tablespoon coconut flakes (sugar-free)

- ❖ 1 tablespoon walnuts, chopped

Frosting:

- ❖ 2 oz. Cream cheese

- ❖ 2 tablespoons butter

- ❖ 2 tablespoons sweetener

- ❖ ½ teaspoon vanilla

Directions:

1. Combine all the chaffle ingredients except coconut flakes and walnuts in a blender.

2. Blend until smooth.

3. Plug your waffle maker in.

4. Add some mixture to the waffle maker.

5. Cook for 3 minutes.

6. Repeat the steps until the remaining batter is used.

7. While letting the chaffles cool, make the frosting by combining all the ingredients.

8. Use a mixer to combine and turn frosting into a fluffy consistency.

9. Spread the frosting on top of the chaffles.

Nutrition: Calories: 127; Total Fat: 13.7g;

Saturated Fat: 9; **Cholesterol**: .9mg

Sodium: 107.3mg; **Potassium**: 457mg

Total Carbohydrates: 5.5g; **Dietary Fiber**: 1.3g

Protein: 5.3g; **Total Sugars**: 1.5g

17. Simple Peanut Butter Chaffle

⚔ **Servings:** 2

🥄 **Preparation Time**: 5 Minutes

⏰ **Cooking Time**: 7-9 Minutes

📋 ## Ingredients:

For the Batter:

- ❖ 4 eggs

- ❖ 2 ounces cream cheese, softened

- ❖ ¼ cup creamy peanut butter

- ❖ 1 teaspoon vanilla extract

- ❖ 2 tablespoons stevia

- ❖ 5 tablespoons almond flour

Other:

❖ 1 tablespoon coconut oil to brush the waffle maker

Directions:

1. Preheat the waffle maker.

2. Add the eggs, cream cheese, and peanut butter to a bowl and stir with a wire whisk until combined.

3. Add the vanilla extract and Stevia and mix until combined.

4. Stir in the almond flour and stir until combined.

5. Brush the heated waffle maker with coconut oil and add a few tablespoons of the batter.

6. Cover and cook for about 7–8 minutes, depending on your waffle maker.

7. Serve and enjoy.

Nutrition: Calories: 291; Fat: 24.9g; Carbs: 5.9g; Sugar: 2; Protein: 12.5g; Sodium: 1mg

18. Beginner Brownies Chaffle

X **Servings**: 2

✎ **Preparation Time**: 10 Minutes

⏰ **Cooking Time**: 5 Minutes

📋 *Ingredients* :

- ❖ 1 cup cheddar cheese

- ❖ 1 tablespoon. cocoa powder

- ❖ ½ teaspoon baking powder

- ❖ 1 Large egg.

- ❖ ¼ cup melted keto chocolate chips for topping

Directions:

1. Preheat dash minutes waffle iron and grease it.

2. Blend all ingredients in a blender until mixed.

3. Pour one teaspoon of cheese into a waffle maker, and then pour the mixture in the center of the greased waffle.

4. Again, sprinkle cheese on the batter.

5. Cover.

6. Cook chaffles for about 4-5 minutes until cooked and crispy.

7. Once chaffles are cooked, remove them.

8. Top with melted chocolate, and enjoy!

Nutrition: Protein:7; Fat:239; Carbohydrates: 14

19. Holidays Chaffles

X **Servings:** 2

✎ **Preparation Time**: 5 Minutes

⏰ **Cooking Time**: 5 Minutes

📋 *Ingredients*:

❖ 1 cup egg whites

❖ 2 teaspoons. Coconut flour

❖ $\frac{1}{2}$ teaspoon Vanilla

❖ 1 teaspoon baking powder

❖ 1 teaspoon baking soda

❖ 1/8 teaspoon cinnamon powder

❖ 1 cup mozzarella cheese, grated

Topping:

- ❖ Cranberries

- ❖ Keto Chocolate sauce

Directions:

1. Make 4 minutes chaffles from the chaffle ingredients.

2. Top with chocolate sauce and cranberries

3. Serve hot and enjoy!

Nutrition: Protein:133; Fat:201; Carbohydrates: 18

20. Coconut & Walnut Chaffles

🍴 **Servings**: 2

🥄 **Preparation Time**: 10 Minutes

⏰ **Cooking Time**: 24 Minutes

📋 *Ingredients* :

- ❖ 4 organic eggs, beaten
- ❖ 4 ounces cream cheese, softened
- ❖ 1 tablespoon butter, melted
- ❖ 4 tablespoons coconut flour
- ❖ 1 tablespoon almond flour
- ❖ 2 tablespoons Erythritol
- ❖ $1\frac{1}{2}$ teaspoons organic baking powder
- ❖ 1 teaspoon organic vanilla extract
- ❖ $\frac{1}{2}$ teaspoon ground cinnamon
- ❖ 1 tablespoon unsweetened coconut, shredded
- ❖ 1 tablespoon walnuts, chopped

Directions:

1. Preheat a mini waffle maker and then grease it.

2. In a blender, place all ingredients and pulse until creamy and smooth.

3. Divide the mixture into eight portions.

4. Place one portion of the mixture into the preheated waffle iron and cook for about 2-3 minutes or until golden brown.

5. Repeat with the remaining mixture.

6. Serve warm.

Nutrition: Calories: 125; Net Carbs: 2.2g; Fat: 10.2g; Saturated Fat: 5.2g; Carbohydrates: 4g; Dietary Fiber: 1.8g; Sugar: 0.4g; Protein: 4.6 g

21. Carrot Chaffles

🍴 **Servings**: 2

🥄 **Preparation Time**: 15 Minutes

⏰ **Cooking Time**: 18 Minutes

📋 *Ingredients*:

❖ ¾ cup almond flour

- ❖ 1 tablespoon walnuts, chopped

- ❖ 2 tablespoons powdered Erythritol

- ❖ 1 teaspoon organic baking powder

- ❖ ½ teaspoon ground cinnamon

- ❖ ½ teaspoon pumpkin pie spice

- ❖ 1 Organic egg, beaten

- ❖ 2 tablespoons heavy whipping cream

- ❖ 2 tablespoons butter, melted

- ❖ ½ cup carrot, peeled and shredded

Directions:

1. Preheat a mini waffle maker and then grease it.

2. In a bowl, place the flour, walnut, Erythritol, cinnamon, baking powder, and spices and mix well.

3. Add the egg, heavy whipping cream, and butter, and mix until well combined.

4. Gently fold in the carrot.

5. Add about three tablespoons of the mixture into the preheated waffle iron and cook for about two and a half or three minutes or until golden brown.

6. Repeat with the remaining mixture.

7. Serve warm.

Nutrition: Calories: 165; Net Carbs: 2.4g; Fat: 14.7g; Saturated Fat: 4.4g; Carbohydrates: 4.4g; Dietary Fiber: 2g; Sugar: 1g; Protein: 1.5g

22. Pumpkin Chaffles

✗ Servings: 2

🖋 Preparation Time: 10 Minutes

⏰ Cooking Time: 12 Minutes

📋 *Ingredients:*

- ❖ 1 Organic egg, beaten
- ❖ ½ cup Mozzarella cheese, shredded
- ❖ 1½ tablespoon homemade pumpkin puree
- ❖ ½ teaspoon Erythritol
- ❖ ½ teaspoon organic vanilla extract
- ❖ ¼ teaspoon pumpkin pie spice

Directions:

1. Preheat a mini waffle maker and then grease it.

2. In a bowl, place all the ingredients and beat until well combined.

3. Place ¼ of the mixture into the preheated waffle iron and cook for about 4-6 minutes or until golden brown.

4. Repeat with the remaining mixture.

5. Serve warm.

Nutrition: Calories: 59; Net Carbs: 1.2g; Fat: 3.5g;

Saturated Fat: 1.5g; Carbohydrates: 1.6g; Dietary Fiber: 0.4g;

Sugar: 0.7g; Protein: 4.9g

23. Pumpkin & Psyllium Husk Chaffles

X **Servings**: 2

🥄 **Preparation Time**: 15 Minutes

⏰ **Cooking Time**: 18 Minutes

📋 Ingredients:

- ❖ 2 Organic eggs
- ❖ ½ cup mozzarella cheese, shredded
- ❖ 1 tablespoon homemade pumpkin puree
- ❖ 2 teaspoons Erythritol
- ❖ ½ teaspoon psyllium husk powder
- ❖ 1/3 teaspoon ground cinnamon
- ❖ A pinch of salt
- ❖ ½ teaspoon organic vanilla extract

Directions:

1. Preheat a mini waffle maker and then grease it.

2. In a bowl, place all ingredients and beat until well combined.

3. Place ¼ of the mixture into the preheated waffle iron and cook for about 3-4 minutes or until golden brown.

4. Repeat with the remaining mixture.

5. Serve warm.

Nutrition: Calories: 46; **Net Carbs**: 0.6g; **Fat**: 2.8g;

Saturated Fat: 1.1g; **Carbohydrates**: 0.8g; **Dietary Fiber**: 0.2g;

Sugar: 0.4g; **Protein**:3.9g

24. Cinnamon Pumpkin Chaffles

✗ **Servings:** 2

🥄 **Preparation Time**: 10 Minutes

⏰ **Cooking Time**: 16 Minutes

📋 Ingredients:

- ❖ 2 Organic eggs
- ❖ 2/3 cup Mozzarella cheese, shredded
- ❖ 3 tablespoons sugar-free pumpkin puree
- ❖ 3 teaspoons almond flour
- ❖ 2 teaspoons granulated Erythritol
- ❖ 2 teaspoons ground cinnamon

Directions:

1. Preheat a mini waffle maker and then grease it.

2. In a medium bowl, place all ingredients, and with a fork, mix until well combined.

68

3. Place half of the mixture into the preheated waffle iron and cook for about four minutes or until golden brown.

4. Repeat with the remaining mixture.

5. Serve warm.

Nutrition: Calories: 63; Net Carbs: 1.4g; Fat: 4g;

Saturated Fat:1.3g; Carbohydrates:2.5g; Dietary Fiber: 1.1g;

Sugar: 0.6g; Protein: 4.3g

25. Spiced Pumpkin Chaffles

✗ Servings: 2

🥄 Preparation Time: 10 Minutes

⏰ Cooking Time: 8 Minutes

📋 Ingredients:

- ❖ 1 Organic egg, beaten
- ❖ ½ cup Mozzarella cheese, shredded
- ❖ 1 tablespoon sugar-free canned solid pumpkin
- ❖ ¼ teaspoon ground cinnamon
- ❖ A pinch of ground cloves
- ❖ A pinch of ground nutmeg
- ❖ A pinch of ground ginger

Directions:

1. Preheat a mini waffle maker and then grease it.

2. In a medium bowl, place all ingredients, and with a fork, mix until well combined.

3. Place half of the mixture into the preheated waffle iron and cook for about 3-4 minutes or until golden brown.

4. Repeat with the remaining mixture.

5. Serve warm.

Nutrition: **Calories**: 56; **Net Carbs**: 1g; **Fat**: 3.5g;

Saturated Fat: 1.5g; **Carbohydrates**: 1.4g; **Dietary Fiber**: 0.4g;

Sugar: 0.5g; **Protein**: 4.9g

26. Italian Seasoning Chaffles

✗ **Servings:** 2

✎ **Preparation Time**: 10 Minutes

⏰ **Cooking Time**: 8 Minutes

📋 Ingredients:

- ❖ ½ cup Mozzarella cheese, shredded
- ❖ 1 tablespoon Parmesan cheese, shredded
- ❖ 1 Organic egg
- ❖ ¾ teaspoon coconut flour
- ❖ ¼ teaspoon organic baking powder
- ❖ 1/8 teaspoon Italian seasoning
- ❖ A pinch of salt

Directions:

1. Preheat a mini waffle maker and then grease it.

2. In a medium bowl, place all ingredients, and with a

fork, mix until well combined.

3. Place half of the mixture into the preheated waffle iron and cook for about 3-4 minutes or until golden brown.

4. Repeat with the remaining mixture.

5. Serve warm.

Nutrition: Calories: 86; Net Carbs: 1.9g; Fat: 5g;

Saturated Fat: 2.6g; **Carbohydrates**: 3.8g

Dietary Fiber: 1.9g; **Sugar**: 0.6g; **Protein:** 6.5g

27. Garlic Herb Blend Seasoning Chaffles

X **Servings**: 2

Preparation Time: 10 Minutes

Cooking Time: 8 Minutes

Ingredients:

- ❖ 1 Large organic egg, beaten
- ❖ ¼ cup Parmesan cheese, shredded
- ❖ ¼ cup Mozzarella cheese, shredded
- ❖ ½ tablespoon butter, melted
- ❖ 1 teaspoon garlic herb blend seasoning
- ❖ Salt, to taste

Directions:

1. Preheat a mini waffle maker and then grease it.

2. In a bowl, place all the ingredients and beat until well combined.

3. Place half of the mixture into the preheated waffle iron and cook for about 3-4 minutes or until golden brown.

4. Repeat with the remaining mixture.

5. Serve warm.

Nutrition: Calories: 115; Net Carbs: 1.1g; Fat: 8.8g; Saturated Fat: 4.7g; **Carbohydrates**: 1.2g; **Dietary Fiber**: 0.1g; Sugar: 0.2g; **Protein:** 8g

28. BBQ Rub Chaffles

Servings: 2

Preparation Time: 5 Minutes

Cooking Time: 20 Minutes

Ingredients:

- ❖ 2 Organic eggs, beaten
- ❖ 1 cup Cheddar cheese, shredded
- ❖ ½ teaspoon BBQ rub
- ❖ ¼ teaspoon organic baking powder

Directions:

1. Preheat a mini waffle maker and then grease it.

2. In a medium bowl, place all ingredients, and with a fork, mix until well combined.

3. Place ¼ of the mixture into the preheated waffle iron and cook for about 5 minutes or until golden brown.

4. Repeat with the remaining mixture.

5. Serve warm.

Nutrition: Calories: 146; **Net Carbs**: 0.7g; **Fat:** 11.6g;

Saturated Fat: 6.6g; **Carbohydrates**: 0.7g; **Dietary Fiber**: 0g;

Sugar: 0.3g; **Protein**: 9.8g

29. Bagel Seasoning Chaffles

✗ **Servings**: 2

✐ **Preparation Time**: 10 Minutes

⏰ **Cooking Time**: 20 Minutes

📋 Ingredients:

- ❖ 1 Large organic egg
- ❖ 1 cup Mozzarella cheese, shredded
- ❖ 1 tablespoon almond flour
- ❖ 1 teaspoon organic baking powder
- ❖ 2 teaspoons bagel seasoning
- ❖ ¼ teaspoon garlic powder
- ❖ ¼ teaspoon onion powder

Directions:

1. Preheat a mini waffle maker and then grease it.

2. In a medium bowl, place all ingredients, and with a

fork, mix until well combined.

3. Place ¼ of the mixture into the preheated waffle iron and cook for about 3-4 minutes or until golden brown.

4. Repeat with the remaining mixture.

5. Serve warm.

Nutrition: Calories: 73; Net Carbs: 2g; Fat: 5.5g;

Saturated Fat: 1.5g; Carbohydrates: 2.3g

Dietary Fiber: 0.3g; Sugar: 0.9g; Protein: 3.7g

30. Rosemary Chaffles

✗ **Servings**: 2

🥄 **Preparation Time**: 5 Minutes

⏰ **Cooking Time**: 8 Minutes

📋 *Ingredients:*

- ❖ 1 Organic egg, beaten
- ❖ ½ cup Cheddar cheese, shredded
- ❖ 1 tablespoon almond flour
- ❖ 1 tablespoon fresh rosemary, chopped
- ❖ A pinch of salt and freshly ground black pepper

Directions:

1. Preheat a mini waffle maker and then grease it.

2. For the chaffles, in a medium bowl, place all ingredients and with a fork, mix until well combined.

3. Place half of the mixture into the preheated waffle iron and cook for about 3-4 minutes or until golden brown.

4. Repeat with the remaining mixture.

5. Serve warm.

Nutrition: Calories: 173; Net Carbs: 1.1g; Fat: 13.7g; Saturated Fat: 6.9g; Carbohydrates: 2.2g; Dietary Fiber: 1.1g; Sugar: 0.4g; Protein: 9.9g

31. Lemony Fresh Herbs Chaffles

✗ **Servings**: 2

🥄 **Preparation Time**: 15 Minutes

⏰ **Cooking Time**: 24 Minutes

📋 *Ingredients:*

- ❖ ½ cup ground flaxseed
- ❖ 2 Organic eggs
- ❖ ½ cup goat cheddar cheese, grated
- ❖ 2-4 tablespoons plain Greek yogurt
- ❖ 1 tablespoon avocado oil
- ❖ ½ teaspoon baking soda
- ❖ 1 teaspoon fresh lemon juice
- ❖ 2 tablespoons fresh chives, minced
- ❖ 1 tablespoon fresh basil, minced
- ❖ ½ tablespoon fresh mint, minced
- ❖ ¼ tablespoon fresh thyme, minced
- ❖ ¼ tablespoon fresh oregano, minced

❖ Salt and freshly ground black pepper, to taste

Directions:

1. Preheat a waffle iron and then grease it.

2. In a medium bowl, place all ingredients, and with a fork, mix until well combined.

3. Divide the mixture into six portions.

4. Place one portion of the mixture into the preheated waffle iron and cook for about four minutes or until golden brown.

5. Repeat with the remaining mixture.

6. Serve warm.

Nutrition: Calories: 117; Net Carbs: 0.9g; Fat: 7.9g; Saturated Fat: 3g; Carbohydrates: 3.7g; Dietary Fiber: 2.8g; Sugar: 0.7g; Protein: 6.4g

32. Peanut Butter & Jam Sandwich Chaffles

🍴 **Servings**: 2

🥄 **Preparation Time**: 10 Minutes

⏰ **Cooking Time**: 8 Minutes

📋 ## Ingredients:

For the Chaffles:

- ❖ 1 Organic egg
- ❖ ½ cup Monterey Jack cheese, shredded
- ❖ 1 tablespoon almond flour

For the Filling:

- ❖ 1 tablespoon peanut butter
- ❖ 1 tablespoon sugar-free Strawberry jam

Directions:

1. Preheat a mini waffle maker and then grease it.

2. For the chaffles, in a medium bowl, add all ingredients, and with a fork, mix until well combined.

3. Place half of the mixture into the preheated waffle iron and cook for about 3-4 minutes.

4. Spread the peanut butter and jam over one chaffle and top with the remaining chaffle.

5. Cut in half and serve.

Nutrition: Calories: 206; Net Carbs: 6.6gFat: 16.7g; Carbohydrates: 2.6g; Dietary Fiber: 0.9g; Sugar: 1.2g; Protein: 11.7g

33. Blueberry Sandwich Chaffles

Servings: 2

Preparation Time: 10 Minutes

Cooking Time: 10 Minutes

Ingredients:

- ❖ 1 Organic egg, beaten
- ❖ ½ cup Cheddar cheese, shredded

For the Filling:

- ❖ 2 tablespoons Erythritol
- ❖ 1 tablespoon butter, softened
- ❖ 1 tablespoon natural peanut butter
- ❖ 2 tablespoons cream cheese, softened
- ❖ ¼ teaspoon organic vanilla extract
- ❖ 2 teaspoons fresh blueberries

Directions:

1. Preheat a mini waffle maker and then grease it.

2. For the chaffles, in a small bowl, add the egg and Cheddar cheese and stir to combine.

3. Place half of the mixture into the preheated waffle iron and cook for about 3-5 minutes.

4. Repeat with the remaining mixture.

5. Meanwhile, for the filling, in a medium bowl, add all ingredients and mix until well combined.

6. Place the filling mixture over one chaffle and top with the remaining chaffle.

7. Cut in half and serve.

Nutrition: Calories: 143; **Net Carbs:** 3.3g; **Fat:** 10.1g; **Carbohydrates:** 4.1g; **Dietary Fiber:** 0.8g; **Sugar:** 1.2g; **Protein:** 7.6g

34. Choco Chip Cannoli Chaffle

🍴 **Servings**: 2

🥄 **Preparation Time**: 10 Minutes

⏰ **Cooking Time**: 20 Minutes

📋 *Ingredients*:

For the Chaffle:

- ❖ 1 egg yolk
- ❖ 1 tablespoon Swerve/Monk fruit
- ❖ 1/8 tablespoon Baking powder
- ❖ 1/8 teaspoon Vanilla extract
- ❖ 3 tablespoons Almond flour
- ❖ 1 tablespoon Chocolate chips

For the Cannoli Topping:

- ✓ 4 tablespoons Cream cheese
- ✓ 6 tablespoons Ricotta

- ✓ 2 tablespoons Sweetener
- ✓ $\frac{1}{4}$ tablespoon Vanilla extract
- ✓ 5 Drops Lemon extract

Directions:

1. Preheat a mini waffle maker and grease it if needed.

2. In a mixing bowl, add all the chaffle ingredients and mix well.

3. Pour the mixture to the lower plate of the waffle maker and spread it evenly to cover the plate properly, and close the lid.

4. Cook for at least 4 minutes to get the desired crunch.

5. In the meanwhile, prepare the cannoli topping by adding all the ingredients to the blender to give the creamy texture.

6. Remove the chaffle from the heat and keep it aside to cool it down.

7. Make as many chaffles as your mixture and waffle

maker allow.

8. Serve with the cannoli toppings and enjoy.

Nutrition: Calories: 159; Fat: 1g Carbohydrates: 34g; Phosphorus: 130mg; Potassium: 116mg; Sodium: 33mg; Protein: 4g

35. Tomato Onions Chaffles

🍴 **Servings**: 2

🥄 **Preparation Time**: 10 Minutes

⏰ **Cooking Time**: 20 Minutes

📋 Ingredients :

For the Chaffle:

- ❖ 1 egg
- ❖ 1/2 cup Mozzarella cheese (shredded)
- ❖ ½ cup chopped onion
- ❖ ½ teaspoon garlic powder
- ❖ ½ teaspoon Dried basil

For the Topping:

- ❖ 1 Large thickly sliced tomato
- ❖ ½ cup (shredded) mozzarella cheese
- ❖ ½ teaspoon oregano

Directions:

1. Preheat a mini waffle maker if needed and grease it.

2. In a mixing bowl, add all the ingredients of the chaffle and mix well.

3. Pour the mixture into the waffle maker.

4. Cook for at least 4 minutes to get the desired crunch, and make as many chaffles as your batter allows.

5. Preheat the oven.

6. Spread the chaffles on the baking sheet and top with one tomato slice.

7. Sprinkle cheese on top and put the baking sheet into the oven.

8. Heat for 5 minutes to melt the cheese.

9. Spread oregano on top and serve hot.

Nutrition: Calories: 175; **Fat:** 10g **Carbohydrates**: 19g;

Phosphorus: 111mg **Potassium:** 170mg; **Sodium**: 62mg;

Protein: 5g

36. Zucchini in Chaffles

🍴 **Servings:** 2

🥄 **Preparation Time**: 10 Minutes

⏰ **Cooking Time**: 18 Minutes

📋 *Ingredients:*

- ❖ 2 large zucchinis, grated and squeezed
- ❖ 2 large organic eggs
- ❖ 2/3 cup Cheddar cheese, shredded
- ❖ 2 tablespoons coconut flour
- ❖ ½ teaspoon garlic powder
- ❖ ½ teaspoon red pepper flakes, crushed
- ❖ Salt, to taste

Directions:

1. Preheat a waffle iron and then grease it.

2. In a medium bowl, place all ingredients and mix until well combined.

3. Place ¼ of the mixture into the preheated waffle iron and cook for about 4-4½ minutes or until golden brown.

4. Repeat with the remaining mixture.

5. Serve warm.

Nutrition: Calories: 311; **Protein:** 16g; **Carbs:** 17g;

Fat: 15g; **Sodium:** (Na) 31mg; **Potassium:** (K) 418mg;

Phosphorus: 257mg

37. 3-Cheese Broccoli Chaffles

✗ **Servings**: 2

🥄 **Preparation Time**: 10 Minutes

⏰ **Cooking Time**: 16 Minutes

📋 ## *Ingredients*:

- ❖ ½ cup cooked broccoli, chopped finely
- ❖ 2 organic eggs, beaten
- ❖ ½ cup Cheddar cheese, shredded
- ❖ ½ cup Mozzarella cheese, shredded
- ❖ 2 tablespoons Parmesan cheese, grated
- ❖ ½ teaspoon onion powder

Directions:

1. Preheat a waffle iron and then grease it.

2. In a bowl, place all ingredients and mix until well combined.

3. Place half of the mixture into the preheated waffle iron and cook for about four minutes or until golden brown.

4. Repeat with the remaining mixture.

5. Serve warm.

Nutrition: Calories: 199; **Protein**: 19g; **Carbs**: 7g;

Fat: 8g; **Sodium**: (Na) 466mg; **Potassium**: (K) 251mg;

Phosphorus: 211mg

38. Plum and Almonds Chaffle

🍴 **Servings**: 2

🥄 **Preparation Time**: 15 Minutes

⏰ **Cooking Time**: 20 Minutes

📋 Ingredients:

- ❖ 1/3 cup cheddar cheese
- ❖ 1 egg
- ❖ 1 tablespoon lemon juice
- ❖ ½ cup puree plum
- ❖ 2 tablespoons almond flour
- ❖ 1/4 teaspoon baking powder
- ❖ 2 tablespoons ground almonds
- ❖ 1/3 cup mozzarella cheese

Directions:

1. Mix cheddar cheese, egg, lemon juice, almond flour, plum, almond ground, and baking powder together in a bowl.

2. Preheat your waffle iron and grease it.

3. In your mini waffle iron, shred half of the mozzarella cheese.

4. Add the mixture to your mini waffle iron.

5. Again, shred the remaining mozzarella cheese on the mixture.

6. Cook till the desired crisp is achieved.

7. Make as many chaffles as your mixture and waffle maker allow.

Nutrition: Calories: 188; **Fat:** 6g; **Carbohydrates:** 33g; **Phosphorus:** 73mg; **Potassium:** 136mg; **Sodium:** 177mg; **Protein:** 4g

39. Easy Blueberry Chaffle

✗ **Servings**: 2

✎ **Preparation Time**: 5 Minutes

⏰ **Cooking Time**: 10 Minutes

📋 *Ingredients*:

- ❖ 2 eggs
- ❖ 2 oz. Cream cheese
- ❖ 2 tablespoons coconut flour
- ❖ 4 teaspoons Swerve/Monk fruit:
- ❖ ½ teaspoon baking powder
- ❖ 1 teaspoon vanilla extract
- ❖ ½ cup blueberries

Directions:

1. Take a small mixing bowl and add Swerve/Monk fruit, baking powder, and coconut flour and mix them all well.

2. Now add the eggs, vanilla extract, and cream cheese,

and beat them all together till uniform consistency is achieved.

3. Preheat a mini waffle maker and grease it if needed.

4. Pour the mixture into the lower plate of the waffle maker.

5. Add 3-4 fresh blueberries above the mixture and close the lid.

6. Cook for at least 4 minutes to get the desired crunch.

7. Remove the chaffle from the heat.

8. Make as many chaffles as your mixture and waffle maker allow.

9. Serve with butter or whipped cream that you like!

Nutrition: Calories: 304; **Fat:** 29g

Carbohydrates: 12g; **Phosphorus**: 119mg

Potassium: 109mg; **Sodium**: 204mg; **Protein**: 9g

40. Dried Herbs Chaffle

✗ **Servings**: 2

✎ **Preparation Time**: 6 Minutes

⏰ **Cooking Time**: 8 Minutes

📋 Ingredients:

- ❖ 1 organic egg, beaten
- ❖ ½ cup Cheddar cheese, shredded
- ❖ 1 tablespoon almond flour
- ❖ A pinch of dried thyme, crushed
- ❖ A pinch of dried rosemary, crushed

Directions:

1. Preheat a mini waffle maker and then grease it.

2. In a bowl, place all the ingredients and beat until well combined.

3. Place half of the mixture into the preheated waffle iron

and cook for about four minutes or until golden brown.

4. Repeat with the remaining mixture.

5. Serve warm.

Nutrition: Calories: 80; Fat: 2.5; Fiber: 3.9

Carbs: 10.9; Protein: 4

41. Zucchini & Basil Chaffles

✗ **Servings**: 2

🥄 **Preparation Time**: 6 Minutes

⏰ **Cooking Time**: 10 Minutes

Ingredients :

- ❖ 1 organic egg, beaten
- ❖ ¼ cup Mozzarella cheese, shredded
- ❖ 2 tablespoons Parmesan cheese, grated
- ❖ ½ of a small zucchini, grated and squeezed
- ❖ ¼ teaspoon dried basil, crushed
- ❖ Freshly ground black pepper, as required

Directions:

1. Preheat a mini waffle maker and then grease it.

2. In a medium bowl, place all ingredients and mix until well combined.

3. Place half of the mixture into the preheated waffle iron and cook for about 4-5 minutes or until golden brown.

4. Repeat with the remaining mixture.

5. Serve warm.

Nutrition: Calories: 43; Fat: 3.4; Fiber: 1.7

Carbs: 3.4; Protein: 1.3

42. Hash Brown Chaffle

Servings: 2

Preparation Time: 6 Minutes

Cooking Time: 10 Minutes

Ingredients:

- ❖ 1 large jicama root, peeled and shredded
- ❖ ½ medium onion, minced
- ❖ 2 garlic cloves, pressed
- ❖ 1 cup cheddar shredded cheese
- ❖ 2 eggs
- ❖ Salt and pepper, to taste

Directions:

1. Place jicama in a colander, sprinkle with two teaspoons salt, and let drain.

2. Squeeze out all excess liquid.

3. Microwave jicama for 5-8 minutes.

4. Mix ¾ of cheese and all other ingredients in a bowl.

5. Sprinkle 1-2 teaspoon cheese on the waffle maker, add three tablespoons of the mixture, and top with 1-2 teaspoon cheese.

6. Cook for 5-minutes, or until done.

7. Remove and repeat for the remaining batter.

8. Serve while hot with your preferred toppings.

Nutrition: Calories: 81; Fat: 4.2; Fiber: 6.5

Carbs: 11.1; Protein: 1.9

43. Ham & Tomato Sandwich Chaffles

🍴 **Servings**: 2

🥄 **Preparation Time**: 10 Minutes

⏰ **Cooking Time**: 8 Minutes

📋 *Ingredients:*

For the Chaffles:

- ❖ 1 organic egg, beaten
- ❖ ½ cup Monterrey Jack cheese, shredded
- ❖ 1 teaspoon coconut flour
- ❖ A pinch of garlic powder

For the Filling:

- ❖ 2 sugar-free ham slices
- ❖ 1 small tomato, sliced
- ❖ 2 lettuce leaves

Directions:

1. Preheat a mini waffle maker and then grease it.

2. For the chaffles, in a medium bowl, add all ingredients, and with a fork, mix until well combined.

3. Place half of the mixture into the preheated waffle iron and cook for about 3-4 minutes.

4. Repeat with the remaining mixture.

5. Place the filling ingredients over one chaffle and top

with the remaining chaffle.

6. Cut in half and serve.

Nutrition: Calories: 156; Net Carbs: 2.7g; Fat: 8.7g;

Carbohydrates: 5.5g; **Dietary Fiber**: 1.8g; **Sugar**: 1.5g;

Protein: 13.9g

44. Smoked Salmon & Cream Sandwich Chaffles

🍴 **Servings:** 2

🥄 **Preparation Time**: 10 Minutes

⏰ **Cooking Time**: 8 Minutes

📋 Ingredients:

For the Chaffles:

- ❖ 1 Organic egg, beaten
- ❖ ½ cup Cheddar cheese, shredded
- ❖ 1 tablespoon almond flour
- ❖ 1 tablespoon fresh rosemary, chopped

For the Filling:

- ❖ ¼ cup smoked salmon
- ❖ 1 teaspoon fresh dill, chopped
- ❖ 2 tablespoons cream

Directions:

1. Preheat a mini waffle maker and then grease it.

2. For the chaffles, in a medium bowl, add all ingredients, and with a fork, mix until well combined.

3. Place half of the mixture into the preheated waffle iron and cook for about 3-4 minutes.

4. Repeat with the remaining mixture.

5. Place the filling ingredients over one chaffle and top with the remaining chaffle.

6. Cut in half and serve.

Nutrition: Calories: 202; Net Carbs: 1.7g; Fat: 15.1g; Carbohydrates: 2.9g; Dietary Fiber: 1.2g; Sugar: 0.7g; Protein: 13.2g

45. Smoked Salmon & Feta Sandwich Chaffles

✗ **Servings**: 2

🥄 **Preparation Time**: 15 Minutes

⏰ **Cooking Time**: 24 Minutes

🗒 *Ingredients*:

For the Chaffles:

- ❖ 2 Organic eggs
- ❖ ½ Ounce butter, melted
- ❖ 1 cup Mozzarella cheese, shredded
- ❖ 2 tablespoons almond flour
- ❖ A pinch of salt

For the Filling:

- ❖ ½ cup smoked salmon
- ❖ 1/3 cup avocado, peeled, pitted, and sliced
- ❖ 2 tablespoons feta cheese, crumbled

Directions:

1. Preheat a mini waffle maker and then grease it.

2. For the chaffles, in a medium bowl, add all ingredients, and with a fork, mix until well combined.

3. Place ¼ of the mixture into the preheated waffle iron and cook for about 5-6 minutes.

4. Repeat with the remaining mixture.

5. Place the filling ingredients over two chaffles and top with the remaining chaffles.

6. Cut each in half and serve.

Nutrition: Calories: 169; **Net Carbs**: 1.2g; **Fat**: 13.5g; Carbohydrates: 2.8g; **Dietary Fiber**: 1.6g; **Sugar**: 1.6g; Protein: 8.9g

46. Cream Cheese Pumpkin Chaffle

✕ **Servings**: 2

🥄 **Preparation Time**: 5 Minutes

⏰ **Cooking Time**: 10 Minutes

📋 *Ingredients*:

- ❖ 2 eggs
- ❖ 2 oz. Cream cheese
- ❖ 2 teaspoons Coconut flour
- ❖ 4 teaspoons Swerve/Monk fruit
- ❖ ½ teaspoon Baking powder
- ❖ 1 teaspoon Vanilla extract
- ❖ 2 tablespoons canned pumpkin
- ❖ ½ teaspoon Pumpkin spice

Directions:

1. Take a small mixing bowl and add Swerve/Monk fruit, coconut flour, and baking powder and mix them all well.

2. Now add the egg, vanilla extract, pumpkin, and cream cheese, and beat them all together till uniform consistency is achieved.

3. Preheat a mini waffle maker if needed.

4. Pour the mixture into the greasy waffle maker.

5. Cook for at least 4 minutes to get the desired crunch.

6. Remove the chaffle from the heat.

7. Make as many chaffles as your mixture and waffle maker allow

8. Serve with butter or whipped cream that you like!

Nutrition: Calories: 197; Fat: 4g

Carbohydrates: 35g; **Phosphorus**: 109mg

Potassium: 192mg; **Sodium**: 159mg; **Protein**: 6g

47. Berries - Coconut Chaffles

X Servings: 2

♪ Preparation Time: 5 Minutes

⏰ Cooking Time: 20 Minutes

📋 *Ingredients* :

- ❖ 1/3 cup Cheddar cheese
- ❖ 1 egg
- ❖ ½ cup Blackberries
- ❖ 2 tablespoons Coconut flour
- ❖ 1/4 teaspoon Baking powder
- ❖ 2 tablespoons coconut flakes
- ❖ 1/3 cup mozzarella cheese

Directions:

1. Mix cheddar cheese, egg, coconut flour, coconut flakes, blackberries, and baking powder together in a bowl

2. Preheat your waffle iron and grease it.

3. In your mini waffle iron, shred half of the mozzarella cheese.

4. Add the mixture to your mini waffle iron.

5. Again, shred the remaining mozzarella cheese on the mixture.

6. Cook till the desired crisp is achieved.

7. Make as many chaffles as your mixture and waffle maker allow.

Nutrition: Calories: 331; Fat: 11g

Carbohydrates: 52g; **Phosphorus**: 90mg

Potassium: 89mg; **Sodium**: 35mg; **Protein**: 6g

48. Sweet & Savory Milky Chaffle

✗ Servings: 2

✎ Preparation Time: 5 Minutes

⏰ Cooking Time: 4 Minutes

📋 *Ingredients*:

- ❖ 3/4 teaspoon baking powder

- ❖ 2 eggs

- ❖ 4 teaspoon heavy whipping cream

- ❖ 1/2 cup coconut milk

- ❖ 1/2 cup mozzarella cheese, shredded

- ❖ 10 Drops Liquid Stevia

- ❖ 1 teaspoon coconut or almond flour

- ❖ 1/2 teaspoon vanilla

Directions:

1. Preheat the mini waffle maker until hot

2. Whisk the eggs in a bowl, add cheese, and then mix well

3. Stir in the remaining ingredients (except toppings, if any).

4. Scoop 1/2 of the batter onto the waffle maker, spread across evenly.

5. Cook 3-4 minutes, until done as desired (or crispy).

6. Gently remove from the waffle maker and let it cool

7. Repeat with the remaining batter.

8. Top with coconut milk and whipping cream.

9. Serve and Enjoy!

Nutrition: Calories: 231; **Net carbs**: 2g; **Fat**: 21g; **Protein**: 12g

49. Sweet Raspberry Chaffle

✗ **Servings**: 2

✎ **Preparation Time**: 5 Minutes

⏰ **Cooking Time**: 5 Minutes

📋 ## Ingredients :

- ❖ 1 teaspoon baking powder

- ❖ 2 eggs

- ❖ 1 cup of mozzarella cheese

- ❖ 2 tablespoons almond flour

- ❖ 4 Raspberries, chopped

- ❖ 1 teaspoon cinnamon

- ❖ 10 Drops Stevia, liquid

Directions:

1. Preheat the mini waffle maker until hot

2. Whisk egg in a bowl, add cheese, and then mix well

3. Stir in the remaining ingredients (except toppings, if any).

4. Grease the preheated waffle maker with non-stick cooking spray.

5. Scoop 1/2 of the batter onto the waffle maker, spread across evenly

6. Cook until a bit browned and crispy, about 4 minutes.

7. Cook 3-4 minutes, until done as desired (or crispy).

8. Gently remove from the waffle maker and let it cool

9. Repeat with the remaining batter.

10. Top with keto syrup

11. Serve and Enjoy!

Nutrition: Calories: 116; Net carbs: 1g; Fat: 8g;

Protein: 8g

50. Savory & Crispy Breakfast Chaffle

✗ **Servings**: 1

✎ **Preparation Time**: 3 Minutes

⏰ **Cooking Time**: 6 Minutes

📋 Ingredients:

- ❖ 2 tablespoons butter

- ❖ 1 egg

- ❖ 1/2 cup Monterey Jack Cheese

- ❖ 1 tablespoon almond flour

Directions:

1. Preheat the mini waffle maker until hot

2. Whisk the egg in a bowl, add cheese, and then mix well

3. Stir in the remaining ingredients (except toppings, if any).

4. Grease waffle maker and Scoop 1/2 of the batter onto the waffle maker, spread across evenly

5. Cook until a bit browned and crispy, about 4 minutes.

6. Gently remove from the waffle maker and let it cool

7. Repeat with the remaining batter.

8. Melt butter in a pan. Add chaffles to the pan and cook for 2 minutes on each side

9. Remove from the pan and let it cool.

10. Serve and Enjoy!

Nutrition: Calories: 257; **Net carbs**: 1g;   **Fat**: 24g;

Protein: 11g

51. Strawberry Shortcake Chaffle

Servings: 2

Preparation Time: 4 Minutes

Cooking Time: 12 Minutes

Ingredients:

Strawberry topping:

- ❖ 3 Fresh strawberries
- ❖ 1/2 tablespoons granulated swerve

Sweet Chaffle Ingredients:

- ❖ 1 tablespoon granulated swerve
- ❖ Keto Whipped Cream
- ❖ 1 tablespoon almond flour
- ❖ 1/2 cup mozzarella cheese
- ❖ 1/4 teaspoon vanilla extract
- ❖ 1 egg

Directions:

1. Preheat the waffle maker until hot

2. Whisk the egg in a bowl, add cheese and then mix well

3. In a small bowl, add the strawberries and swerve, mix until well-combined. Set aside.

4. In another bowl, add the "sweet chaffle ingredients" and mix thoroughly.

5. Pour 1/3 of the batter into your mini waffle maker and cook for 3-4 minutes.

6. Rove gently and set aside to cool

7. Repeat for the remaining batter, make three chaffle cakes in total.

8. Assemble the Chaffle by topping with strawberries and whipped cream.

9. Serve and Enjoy!

Nutrition: Calories: 112; Net carbs: 1g; Fat: 8g;

Protein: 7g

CONCLUSION

The ketogenic diet is an incredibly great way to lose weight and get rid of the fat layers around your arms, legs, stomach, and even your internal organs. The results of the burned fat are visible within a couple of weeks (if you stick to the recommended foods and don't cheat).

Weight loss is one of the most popular reasons why people start this diet is because it is a sure way to lose weight and not face the yo-yo effect. It is because the keto diet offers a plethora of delicious foods and recipes that will keep you full and kill off your cravings for junk food and food rich in carbs or sugar.

Nutritionists and doctors often recommend it to overweight people who must lose weight, not for aesthetic reasons but because their life and health are in danger. This diet is great even if you don't want to lose weight. Just switch to keto meals, and you will lower the risk of many nasty diseases. Also, you will eat healthy and balanced food free of excessive amounts of sodium, sugar, carbs, and unhealthy oils and fats. As your body increases the ketone levels, all the stored fats will turn into energy. So, the gain is double—weight and fat loss, and a healthy and energized body.

The anti-inflammatory effect is true. No matter how crazy it sounds, once you start following the keto diet and the ketones in your body increase and fats are the primary energy source, you will release less reactive oxygen species and free radicals, which are dangerous for any human being. Free radicals and reactive oxygen species are the main reasons why today, people are more prone to deadly illnesses such as cancer. The less sugar you consume, the lower the risk is for you to develop inflammatory processes of any kind, to put it simply.

The diet helps decrease sugar levels in the blood. The more carbohydrates you eat, the more they are turned into blood sugar. You do not have to be a doctor to know that high blood sugar levels are the main reason why the insulin in the body rises. Increased insulin levels are the main reason for type 2 diabetes. Since this diet recommends foods that are deficient in carbohydrates, your body becomes supplied with a high level of fats, which have now become its primary energy source.

The fats you consume, and the fats that have already been stored are slowly burned and turned into energy for your brain. As the liver transforms the fats into ketones, there is a low level of insulin in the body. You are in control of insulin levels and prevent yourself from the risk of diabetes. If you have this condition, then you are controlling the insulin and prevent it from growing higher and damaging your health.

The diet helps to have better brain activity; there are far more benefits with the keto diet than weight loss, dropped levels of insulin in your body. You will feel more energized, but also low-carb food will put your brain in better shape. Now, if you are a young person, perhaps you don't think that this is necessary for you, but improved brain activity is super important for older people. No matter if you are a young or older person, the keto diet will improve your memory, and you will have an easier time learning and understanding new things. The great thing is that you will have an easier time keeping your thoughts in a better state, and your mood swings will significantly improve.

Lightning Source UK Ltd.
Milton Keynes UK
UKHW020747250621
386136UK00005B/30